# BUCKET LIST JOURNAL

A list of things I want to do in my lifetime

These are some themes that you could use for your goals / activities on your Bucket List. Use these as prompts for you to think about the things that you want to achieve in your lifetime.

1. **Travel:** What countries and places do you want to visit?

2. **Adventure:** What adventures and thrill seeking activities do you want to experience?

3. **Career:** What do you want to accomplish in your career? What industry do you want to work in?

4. **Finance:** What financial goals do you have?

5. **Relationships:** Is there something that you want to get out of the relationship that you are in or do you want to experience something with a special person?

6. **Personal Development:** What new things do you want to learn that can develop you on a personal level?

7. **Community:** Things you might want to achieve in your local community. What groups or activities do you want to take part in?

| Bucket List Goal | Target Date | ✓ Done |
|---|---|---|
| 1 | | ☐ |
| 2 | | ☐ |
| 3 | | ☐ |
| 4 | | ☐ |
| 5 | | ☐ |
| 6 | | ☐ |
| 7 | | ☐ |
| 8 | | ☐ |
| 9 | | ☐ |
| 10 | | ☐ |

| Bucket List Goal | Target Date | ✓ Done |
|---|---|---|
| 11 | | |
| 12 | | |
| 13 | | |
| 14 | | |
| 15 | | |
| 16 | | |
| 17 | | |
| 18 | | |
| 19 | | |
| 20 | | |

| Bucket List Goal | Target Date | ✓ Done |
|---|---|---|
| 21 | | ☐ |
| 22 | | ☐ |
| 23 | | ☐ |
| 24 | | ☐ |
| 25 | | ☐ |
| 26 | | ☐ |
| 27 | | ☐ |
| 28 | | ☐ |
| 29 | | ☐ |
| 30 | | ☐ |

| Bucket List Goal | Target Date | ✓ Done |
|---|---|---|
| 31 | | ☐ |
| 32 | | ☐ |
| 33 | | ☐ |
| 34 | | ☐ |
| 35 | | ☐ |
| 36 | | ☐ |
| 37 | | ☐ |
| 38 | | ☐ |
| 39 | | ☐ |
| 40 | | ☐ |

| Bucket List Goal | Target Date | ✓ Done |
|---|---|---|
| 41 | | ☐ |
| 42 | | ☐ |
| 43 | | ☐ |
| 44 | | ☐ |
| 45 | | ☐ |
| 46 | | ☐ |
| 47 | | ☐ |
| 48 | | ☐ |
| 49 | | ☐ |
| 50 | | ☐ |

| Bucket List Goal | Target Date | ✓ Done |
|---|---|---|
| 51 | | |
| 52 | | |
| 53 | | |
| 54 | | |
| 55 | | |
| 56 | | |
| 57 | | |
| 58 | | |
| 59 | | |
| 60 | | |

| Bucket List Goal | Target Date | ✓ Done |
|---|---|---|
| 61 | | |
| 62 | | |
| 63 | | |
| 64 | | |
| 65 | | |
| 66 | | |
| 67 | | |
| 68 | | |
| 69 | | |
| 70 | | |

| Bucket List Goal | Target Date | ✓ Done |
|---|---|---|
| 71 | | |
| 72 | | |
| 73 | | |
| 74 | | |
| 75 | | |
| 76 | | |
| 77 | | |
| 78 | | |
| 79 | | |
| 80 | | |

| Bucket List Goal | Target Date | ✓ Done |
|---|---|---|
| 81 | | |
| 82 | | |
| 83 | | |
| 84 | | |
| 85 | | |
| 86 | | |
| 87 | | |
| 88 | | |
| 89 | | |
| 90 | | |

| Bucket List Goal | Target Date | ✓ Done |
|---|---|---|
| 91 | | |
| 92 | | |
| 93 | | |
| 94 | | |
| 95 | | |
| 96 | | |
| 97 | | |
| 98 | | |
| 99 | | |
| 100 | | |

## Bucket List Goal

Target Date

Why I want to do this

Resources needed

Notes

Goal Achieved

Yes ☐  No ☐

Your Overall
Satisfaction Rating
Mark out of 10)

1 2 3 4 5 6 7 8 9 10

## Bucket List Goal

Target Date

*Why I want to do this*

*Resources needed*

*Notes*

*Goal Achieved*

Yes ☐       No ☐

*Your Overall Satisfaction Rating (Mark out of 10)*

**1 2 3 4 5 6 7 8 9 10**

**Bucket List Goal**

*Target Date*

*Why I want to do this*

*Resources needed*

*Notes*

*Goal Achieved*

Yes ☐       No ☐

*Your Overall Satisfaction Rating (Mark out of 10)*

1 2 3 4 5 6 7 8 9 10

**Bucket List Goal**

*Target Date*

*Why I want to do this*

*Resources needed*

*Notes*

*Goal Achieved*

Yes        No

*Your Overall Satisfaction Rating (Mark out of 10)*

1 2 3 4 5 6 7 8 9 10

## Bucket List Goal

Target Date

**Why I want to do this**

**Resources needed**

Notes

Goal Achieved

Yes ☐       No ☐

Your Overall
Satisfaction Rating
(Mark out of 10)

1 2 3 4 5 6 7 8 9 10

## Bucket List Goal

*Target Date*

*Why I want to do this*

*Resources needed*

*Notes*

*Goal Achieved*

Yes ☐     No ☐

*Your Overall Satisfaction Rating (Mark out of 10)*

1 2 3 4 5 6 7 8 9 10

**Bucket List Goal**

*Target Date*

*Why I want to do this*

*Resources needed*

*Notes*

*Goal Achieved*

Yes ☐ No ☐

*Your Overall Satisfaction Rating (Mark out of 10)*

1 2 3 4 5 6 7 8 9 10

## Bucket List Goal

Target Date

Why I want to do this

Resources needed

Notes

Goal Achieved

Yes ☐          No ☐

Your Overall
Satisfaction Rating
(Mark out of 10)

1 2 3 4 5 6 7 8 9 10

## Bucket List Goal

*Target Date*

*Why I want to do this*

*Resources needed*

*Notes*

*Goal Achieved*

Yes ☐          No ☐

*Your Overall*
*Satisfaction Rating*
*(Mark out of 10)*

1 2 3 4 5 6 7 8 9 10

**Bucket List Goal**

*Target Date*

*Why I want to do this*

*Resources needed*

*Notes*

*Goal Achieved*

Yes ☐     No ☐

*Your Overall Satisfaction Rating (Mark out of 10)*

1 2 3 4 5 6 7 8 9 10

## Bucket List Goal

**Target Date**

**Why I want to do this**

**Resources needed**

**Notes**

**Goal Achieved**

Yes ☐     No ☐

**Your Overall Satisfaction Rating (Mark out of 10)**

1 2 3 4 5 6 7 8 9 10

## Bucket List Goal

*Target Date*

*Why I want to do this*

*Resources needed*

*Notes*

*Goal Achieved*

Yes ☐　　　　No ☐

*Your Overall Satisfaction Rating (Mark out of 10)*

1 2 3 4 5 6 7 8 9 10

## Bucket List Goal

*Target Date*

*Why I want to do this*

*Resources needed*

*Notes*

*Goal Achieved*

Yes ☐                    No ☐

*Your Overall Satisfaction Rating (Mark out of 10)*

1 2 3 4 5 6 7 8 9 10

**Bucket List Goal**

*Target Date*

*Why I want to do this*

*Resources needed*

*Notes*

*Goal Achieved*

Yes        No

*Your Overall Satisfaction Rating (Mark out of 10)*

1 2 3 4 5 6 7 8 9 10

## Bucket List Goal

Target Date

Why I want to do this

Resources needed

Notes

Goal Achieved

Yes ☐     No ☐

Your Overall
Satisfaction Rating
(Mark out of 10)

1 2 3 4 5 6 7 8 9 10

## Bucket List Goal

[ ]

*Target Date*

[ ]

*Why I want to do this*

*Resources needed*

*Notes*

*Goal Achieved*

Yes [ ]    No [ ]

*Your Overall
Satisfaction Rating
(Mark out of 10)*

1 2 3 4 5 6 7 8 9 10

## Bucket List Goal

**Target Date**

*Why I want to do this*

*Resources needed*

*Notes*

*Goal Achieved*

Yes ☐          No ☐

*Your Overall Satisfaction Rating (Mark out of 10)*

1  2  3  4  5  6  7  8  9  10

## Bucket List Goal

Target Date

*Why I want to do this*

*Resources needed*

*Notes*

*Goal Achieved*

Yes ☐          No ☐

*Your Overall
Satisfaction Rating
(Mark out of 10)*

1 2 3 4 5 6 7 8 9 10

**Bucket List Goal**

*Target Date*

*Why I want to do this*

*Resources needed*

*Notes*

*Goal Achieved*

Yes ☐    No ☐

*Your Overall Satisfaction Rating (Mark out of 10)*

1 2 3 4 5 6 7 8 9 10

**Bucket List Goal**

*Target Date*

*Why I want to do this*

*Resources needed*

*Notes*

*Goal Achieved*

Yes ☐                    No ☐

*Your Overall Satisfaction Rating (Mark out of 10)*

1  2  3  4  5  6  7  8  9  10

## Bucket List Goal

*Target Date*

*Why I want to do this*

*Resources needed*

*Notes*

*Goal Achieved*

Yes ☐  No ☐

*Your Overall*
*Satisfaction Rating*
*(Mark out of 10)*

**1 2 3 4 5 6 7 8 9 10**

**Bucket List Goal**

*Target Date*

*Why I want to do this*

*Resources needed*

*Notes*

*Goal Achieved*

Yes ☐                No ☐

*Your Overall
Satisfaction Rating
(Mark out of 10)*

1 2 3 4 5 6 7 8 9 10

**Bucket List Goal**

*Target Date*

*Why I want to do this*

*Resources needed*

*Notes*

*Goal Achieved*

Yes ☐          No ☐

*Your Overall Satisfaction Rating (Mark out of 10)*

1 2 3 4 5 6 7 8 9 10

## Bucket List Goal

Target Date

*Why I want to do this*

*Resources needed*

*Notes*

*Goal Achieved*

Yes ☐          No ☐

*Your Overall Satisfaction Rating (Mark out of 10)*

1  2  3  4  5  6  7  8  9  10

**Bucket List Goal**

*Target Date*

*Why I want to do this*

*Resources needed*

*Notes*

*Goal Achieved*

Yes ☐     No ☐

*Your Overall Satisfaction Rating (Mark out of 10)*

1 2 3 4 5 6 7 8 9 10

# Bucket List Goal

**Target Date**

## Why I want to do this

## Resources needed

## Notes

**Goal Achieved**

Yes ☐     No ☐

**Your Overall Satisfaction Rating (Mark out of 10)**

1 2 3 4 5 6 7 8 9 10

## Bucket List Goal

**Target Date**

**Why I want to do this**

**Resources needed**

**Notes**

**Goal Achieved**

Yes ☐　　　No ☐

**Your Overall Satisfaction Rating (Mark out of 10)**

1 2 3 4 5 6 7 8 9 10

## Bucket List Goal

Target Date

*Why I want to do this*

*Resources needed*

*Notes*

*Goal Achieved*

Yes ☐ No ☐

*Your Overall
Satisfaction Rating
(Mark out of 10)*

1 2 3 4 5 6 7 8 9 10

## Bucket List Goal

Target Date

Why I want to do this

Resources needed

Notes

Goal Achieved

Yes  No

Your Overall
Satisfaction Rating
(Mark out of 10)

1 2 3 4 5 6 7 8 9 10

# Bucket List Goal

Target Date

Why I want to do this

Resources needed

Notes

Goal Achieved

Yes ☐    No ☐

Your Overall
Satisfaction Rating
(Mark out of 10)

1 2 3 4 5 6 7 8 9 10

**Bucket List Goal**

*Target Date*

*Why I want to do this*

*Resources needed*

*Notes*

*Goal Achieved*

Yes ☐          No ☐

*Your Overall Satisfaction Rating (Mark out of 10)*

1 2 3 4 5 6 7 8 9 10

## Bucket List Goal

Target Date

*Why I want to do this*

*Resources needed*

*Notes*

*Goal Achieved*

Yes ☐          No ☐

*Your Overall
Satisfaction Rating
(Mark out of 10)*

1 2 3 4 5 6 7 8 9 10

**Bucket List Goal**

*Target Date*

*Why I want to do this*

*Resources needed*

*Notes*

*Goal Achieved*

Yes ☐          No ☐

*Your Overall
Satisfaction Rating
(Mark out of 10)*

1 2 3 4 5 6 7 8 9 10

**Bucket List Goal**

*Target Date*

*Why I want to do this*

*Resources needed*

*Notes*

*Goal Achieved*

Yes ☐     No ☐

*Your Overall Satisfaction Rating (Mark out of 10)*

1 2 3 4 5 6 7 8 9 10

## Bucket List Goal

Target Date

### Why I want to do this

### Resources needed

### Notes

Goal Achieved

Yes ☐          No ☐

Your Overall
Satisfaction Rating
(Mark out of 10)

1 2 3 4 5 6 7 8 9 10

## Bucket List Goal

*Target Date*

*Why I want to do this*

*Resources needed*

*Notes*

*Goal Achieved*

Yes ☐ No ☐

*Your Overall Satisfaction Rating (Mark out of 10)*

1 2 3 4 5 6 7 8 9 10

**Bucket List Goal**

*Target Date*

*Why I want to do this*

*Resources needed*

*Notes*

*Goal Achieved*

Yes ☐          No ☐

*Your Overall
Satisfaction Rating
(Mark out of 10)*

1 2 3 4 5 6 7 8 9 10

**Bucket List Goal**

*Target Date*

*Why I want to do this*

*Resources needed*

*Notes*

*Goal Achieved*

Yes ☐          No ☐

*Your Overall Satisfaction Rating (Mark out of 10)*

1 2 3 4 5 6 7 8 9 10

## Bucket List Goal

Target Date

Why I want to do this

Resources needed

Notes

Goal Achieved

Yes ☐          No ☐

Your Overall
Satisfaction Rating
(Mark out of 10)

1 2 3 4 5 6 7 8 9 10

**Bucket List Goal**

*Target Date*

*Why I want to do this*

*Resources needed*

*Notes*

*Goal Achieved*

Yes ☐          No ☐

*Your Overall Satisfaction Rating (Mark out of 10)*

1 2 3 4 5 6 7 8 9 10

## Bucket List Goal

*Target Date*

*Why I want to do this*

*Resources needed*

*Notes*

*Goal Achieved*

Yes [ ]    No [ ]

*Your Overall Satisfaction Rating (Mark out of 10)*

1 2 3 4 5 6 7 8 9 10

**Bucket List Goal**

*Target Date*

*Why I want to do this*

*Resources needed*

*Notes*

*Goal Achieved*

Yes ☐          No ☐

*Your Overall
Satisfaction Rating
(Mark out of 10)*

1 2 3 4 5 6 7 8 9 10

## Bucket List Goal

Target Date

Why I want to do this

Resources needed

Notes

Goal Achieved

Yes ☐          No ☐

Your Overall
Satisfaction Rating
(Mark out of 10)

1 2 3 4 5 6 7 8 9 10

## Bucket List Goal

Target Date

*Why I want to do this*

*Resources needed*

*Notes*

*Goal Achieved*

Yes ☐          No ☐

*Your Overall
Satisfaction Rating
(Mark out of 10)*

1  2  3  4  5  6  7  8  9  10

**Bucket List Goal**

*Target Date*

*Why I want to do this*

*Resources needed*

*Notes*

*Goal Achieved*

Yes ☐          No ☐

*Your Overall
Satisfaction Rating
(Mark out of 10)*

1  2  3  4  5  6  7  8  9  10

**Bucket List Goal**

Target Date

Why I want to do this

Resources needed

Notes

Goal Achieved

Yes        No

Your Overall
Satisfaction Rating
(Mark out of 10)

1 2 3 4 5 6 7 8 9 10

**Bucket List Goal**

Target Date

Why I want to do this

Resources needed

Notes

Goal Achieved

Yes ☐ No ☐

Your Overall
Satisfaction Rating
(Mark out of 10)

1 2 3 4 5 6 7 8 9 10

## Bucket List Goal

**Target Date**

### Why I want to do this

### Resources needed

### Notes

**Goal Achieved**

Yes ☐ No ☐

**Your Overall Satisfaction Rating (Mark out of 10)**

1 2 3 4 5 6 7 8 9 10

**Bucket List Goal**

Target Date

Why I want to do this

Resources needed

Notes

Goal Achieved

Yes ☐          No ☐

Your Overall
Satisfaction Rating
(Mark out of 10)

1 2 3 4 5 6 7 8 9 10

**Bucket List Goal**

Target Date

Why I want to do this

Resources needed

Notes

Goal Achieved

Yes          No

Your Overall
Satisfaction Rating
(Mark out of 10)

1 2 3 4 5 6 7 8 9 10

**Bucket List Goal**

*Target Date*

*Why I want to do this*

*Resources needed*

*Notes*

*Goal Achieved*

Yes ☐ No ☐

*Your Overall Satisfaction Rating (Mark out of 10)*

1 2 3 4 5 6 7 8 9 10

**Bucket List Goal**

Target Date

Why I want to do this

Resources needed

Notes

Goal Achieved

Yes ☐          No ☐

Your Overall
Satisfaction Rating
(Mark out of 10)

1 2 3 4 5 6 7 8 9 10

**Bucket List Goal**

*Target Date*

*Why I want to do this*

*Resources needed*

*Notes*

*Goal Achieved*

Yes ☐          No ☐

*Your Overall Satisfaction Rating (Mark out of 10)*

1 2 3 4 5 6 7 8 9 10

**Bucket List Goal**

Target Date

Why I want to do this

Resources needed

Notes

Goal Achieved

Yes ☐    No ☐

Your Overall
Satisfaction Rating
(Mark out of 10)

1 2 3 4 5 6 7 8 9 10

**Bucket List Goal**

Target Date

Why I want to do this

Resources needed

Notes

Goal Achieved

Yes ☐          No ☐

Your Overall
Satisfaction Rating
(Mark out of 10)

1 2 3 4 5 6 7 8 9 10

**Bucket List Goal**

Target Date

Why I want to do this

Resources needed

Notes

Goal Achieved

Yes ☐ No ☐

Your Overall
Satisfaction Rating
(Mark out of 10)

1 2 3 4 5 6 7 8 9 10

**Bucket List Goal**

Target Date

Why I want to do this

Resources needed

Notes

Goal Achieved

Yes ☐          No ☐

Your Overall
Satisfaction Rating
(Mark out of 10)

1 2 3 4 5 6 7 8 9 10

## Bucket List Goal

Target Date

Why I want to do this

Resources needed

Notes

Goal Achieved

Yes    No

Your Overall
Satisfaction Rating
(Mark out of 10)

1 2 3 4 5 6 7 8 9 10

## Bucket List Goal

Target Date

*Why I want to do this*

*Resources needed*

*Notes*

*Goal Achieved*

Yes ☐          No ☐

*Your Overall Satisfaction Rating (Mark out of 10)*

1 2 3 4 5 6 7 8 9 10

**Bucket List Goal**

Target Date

Why I want to do this

Resources needed

Notes

Goal Achieved

Yes ☐ No ☐

Your Overall
Satisfaction Rating
(Mark out of 10)

1 2 3 4 5 6 7 8 9 10

**Bucket List Goal**

Target Date

Why I want to do this

Resources needed

Notes

Goal Achieved

Yes          No

Your Overall
Satisfaction Rating
(Mark out of 10)

1 2 3 4 5 6 7 8 9 10

**Bucket List Goal**

Target Date

Why I want to do this

Resources needed

Notes

Goal Achieved

Yes ☐ No ☐

Your Overall
Satisfaction Rating
(Mark out of 10)

1 2 3 4 5 6 7 8 9 10

**Bucket List Goal**

Target Date

Why I want to do this

Resources needed

Notes

Goal Achieved

Yes ☐          No ☐

Your Overall
Satisfaction Rating
(Mark out of 10)

1 2 3 4 5 6 7 8 9 10

## Bucket List Goal

Target Date

### Why I want to do this

### Resources needed

### Notes

Goal Achieved

Yes ☐     No ☐

Your Overall
Satisfaction Rating
(Mark out of 10)

1 2 3 4 5 6 7 8 9 10

**Bucket List Goal**

Target Date

Why I want to do this

Resources needed

Notes

Goal Achieved

Yes ☐　　　　No ☐

Your Overall
Satisfaction Rating
(Mark out of 10)

1 2 3 4 5 6 7 8 9 10

## Bucket List Goal

Target Date

### Why I want to do this

### Resources needed

### Notes

Goal Achieved

Yes      No

Your Overall
Satisfaction Rating
(Mark out of 10)

1 2 3 4 5 6 7 8 9 10

**Bucket List Goal**

_Target Date_

_Why I want to do this_

_Resources needed_

_Notes_

_Goal Achieved_

Yes ☐          No ☐

_Your Overall_
_Satisfaction Rating_
_(Mark out of 10)_

1 2 3 4 5 6 7 8 9 10

**Bucket List Goal**

*Target Date*

*Why I want to do this*

*Resources needed*

*Notes*

*Goal Achieved*

Yes ☐    No ☐

*Your Overall Satisfaction Rating (Mark out of 10)*

1 2 3 4 5 6 7 8 9 10

**Bucket List Goal**

Target Date

Why I want to do this

Resources needed

Notes

Goal Achieved

Yes [ ]     No [ ]

Your Overall
Satisfaction Rating
(Mark out of 10)

1 2 3 4 5 6 7 8 9 10

## Bucket List Goal

Target Date

Why I want to do this

Resources needed

Notes

Goal Achieved

Yes ☐          No ☐

Your Overall
Satisfaction Rating
(Mark out of 10)

1 2 3 4 5 6 7 8 9 10

## Bucket List Goal

Target Date

Why I want to do this

Resources needed

Notes

Goal Achieved

Yes      No

Your Overall
Satisfaction Rating
(Mark out of 10)

1 2 3 4 5 6 7 8 9 10

**Bucket List Goal**

Target Date

Why I want to do this

Resources needed

Notes

Goal Achieved

Yes ☐　　　　No ☐

Your Overall
Satisfaction Rating
(Mark out of 10)

1 2 3 4 5 6 7 8 9 10

## Bucket List Goal

Target Date

*Why I want to do this*

*Resources needed*

*Notes*

*Goal Achieved*

Yes ☐          No ☐

*Your Overall
Satisfaction Rating
(Mark out of 10)*

1 2 3 4 5 6 7 8 9 10

## Bucket List Goal

**Target Date**

Why I want to do this

Resources needed

Notes

Goal Achieved

Yes   No

Your Overall
Satisfaction Rating
(Mark out of 10)

1  2  3  4  5  6  7  8  9  10

**Bucket List Goal**

Target Date

Why I want to do this

Resources needed

Notes

Goal Achieved

Yes ☐    No ☐

Your Overall
Satisfaction Rating
(Mark out of 10)

1 2 3 4 5 6 7 8 9 10

## Bucket List Goal

Target Date

### Why I want to do this

### Resources needed

### Notes

Goal Achieved

Yes ☐     No ☐

Your Overall
Satisfaction Rating
(Mark out of 10)

1 2 3 4 5 6 7 8 9 10

**Bucket List Goal**

Target Date

Why I want to do this

Resources needed

Notes

Goal Achieved

Yes ☐          No ☐

Your Overall
Satisfaction Rating
(Mark out of 10)

1 2 3 4 5 6 7 8 9 10

## Bucket List Goal

[ ]

*Target Date*

[ ]

*Why I want to do this*

*Resources needed*

*Notes*

*Goal Achieved*

Yes [ ]     No [ ]

*Your Overall
Satisfaction Rating
(Mark out of 10)*

1  2  3  4  5  6  7  8  9  10

**Bucket List Goal**

Target Date

Why I want to do this

Resources needed

Notes

Goal Achieved

Yes    No

Your Overall
Satisfaction Rating
(Mark out of 10)

1 2 3 4 5 6 7 8 9 10

# Bucket List Goal

_Target Date_

_Why I want to do this_

_Resources needed_

_Notes_

_Goal Achieved_

Yes ☐     No ☐

_Your Overall Satisfaction Rating (Mark out of 10)_

1 2 3 4 5 6 7 8 9 10

**Bucket List Goal**

Target Date

Why I want to do this

Resources needed

Notes

Goal Achieved

Yes ☐　　　　No ☐

Your Overall
Satisfaction Rating
(Mark out of 10)

1　2　3　4　5　6　7　8　9　10

## Bucket List Goal

Target Date

Why I want to do this

Resources needed

Notes

Goal Achieved

Yes ☐     No ☐

Your Overall
Satisfaction Rating
(Mark out of 10)

1 2 3 4 5 6 7 8 9 10

## Bucket List Goal

Target Date

### Why I want to do this

### Resources needed

### Notes

Goal Achieved

Yes          No

Your Overall
Satisfaction Rating
(Mark out of 10)

1 2 3 4 5 6 7 8 9 10

## Bucket List Goal

Target Date

### Why I want to do this

### Resources needed

### Notes

Goal Achieved

Yes ☐     No ☐

Your Overall
Satisfaction Rating
(Mark out of 10)

1 2 3 4 5 6 7 8 9 10

**Bucket List Goal**

Target Date

Why I want to do this

Resources needed

Notes

Goal Achieved

Yes ☐          No ☐

Your Overall
Satisfaction Rating
(Mark out of 10)

1 2 3 4 5 6 7 8 9 10

**Bucket List Goal**

*Target Date*

*Why I want to do this*

*Resources needed*

*Notes*

*Goal Achieved*

Yes ☐     No ☐

*Your Overall Satisfaction Rating (Mark out of 10)*

1 2 3 4 5 6 7 8 9 10

**Bucket List Goal**

Target Date

Why I want to do this

Resources needed

Notes

Goal Achieved

Yes ☐     No ☐

Your Overall
Satisfaction Rating
(Mark out of 10)

1 2 3 4 5 6 7 8 9 10

**Bucket List Goal**

Target Date

Why I want to do this

Resources needed

Notes

Goal Achieved

Yes ☐  No ☐

Your Overall
Satisfaction Rating
(Mark out of 10)

1 2 3 4 5 6 7 8 9 10

**Bucket List Goal**

Target Date

Why I want to do this

Resources needed

Notes

Goal Achieved

Yes ☐     No ☐

Your Overall
Satisfaction Rating
(Mark out of 10)

1 2 3 4 5 6 7 8 9 10

**Bucket List Goal**

*Target Date*

*Why I want to do this*

*Resources needed*

*Notes*

*Goal Achieved*

Yes ☐          No ☐

*Your Overall
Satisfaction Rating
(Mark out of 10)*

1 2 3 4 5 6 7 8 9 10

**Bucket List Goal**

Target Date

Why I want to do this

Resources needed

Notes

Goal Achieved

Yes ☐          No ☐

Your Overall
Satisfaction Rating
(Mark out of 10)

1 2 3 4 5 6 7 8 9 10

**Bucket List Goal**

*Target Date*

*Why I want to do this*

*Resources needed*

*Notes*

*Goal Achieved*

Yes ☐          No ☐

*Your Overall
Satisfaction Rating
(Mark out of 10)*

1 2 3 4 5 6 7 8 9 10

**Bucket List Goal**

Target Date

Why I want to do this

Resources needed

Notes

Goal Achieved

Yes ☐          No ☐

Your Overall
Satisfaction Rating
(Mark out of 10)

1 2 3 4 5 6 7 8 9 10

**Bucket List Goal**

*Target Date*

*Why I want to do this*

*Resources needed*

*Notes*

*Goal Achieved*

Yes ☐          No ☐

*Your Overall Satisfaction Rating (Mark out of 10)*

1 2 3 4 5 6 7 8 9 10

**Bucket List Goal**

*Target Date*

*Why I want to do this*

*Resources needed*

*Notes*

*Goal Achieved*

Yes ☐      No ☐

*Your Overall
Satisfaction Rating
(Mark out of 10)*

1 2 3 4 5 6 7 8 9 10

**Bucket List Goal**

Target Date

Why I want to do this

Resources needed

Notes

Goal Achieved

Yes ☐          No ☐

Your Overall
Satisfaction Rating
(Mark out of 10)

1  2  3  4  5  6  7  8  9  10

**Bucket List Goal**

Target Date

Why I want to do this

Resources needed

Notes

Goal Achieved

Yes       No

Your Overall
Satisfaction Rating
(Mark out of 10)

1 2 3 4 5 6 7 8 9 10

## Bucket List Goal

Target Date

### Why I want to do this

### Resources needed

### Notes

Goal Achieved

Yes ☐    No ☐

Your Overall
Satisfaction Rating
(Mark out of 10)

1 2 3 4 5 6 7 8 9 10

**Bucket List Goal**

Target Date

Why I want to do this

Resources needed

Notes

Goal Achieved

Yes ☐          No ☐

Your Overall
Satisfaction Rating
(Mark out of 10)

1 2 3 4 5 6 7 8 9 10

## Bucket List Goal

Target Date

**Why I want to do this**

**Resources needed**

**Notes**

Goal Achieved

Yes ☐ No ☐

Your Overall
Satisfaction Rating
(Mark out of 10)

1 2 3 4 5 6 7 8 9 10

**Bucket List Goal**

Target Date

Why I want to do this

Resources needed

Notes

Goal Achieved

Yes ☐　　　　No ☐

Your Overall
Satisfaction Rating
(Mark out of 10)

1 2 3 4 5 6 7 8 9 10

Made in the USA
San Bernardino, CA
15 December 2014